AF716457

POP BUCHANAN

Invest AI Quantum Computing Stacks

Top Quantum Computing Stack Companies Shaping the Future of AI and Long-Term Investments

Copyright © 2026 by POP Buchanan

All rights reserved. No part of this publication may be reproduced, stored or transmitted in any form or by any means, electronic, mechanical, photocopying, recording, scanning, or otherwise without written permission from the publisher. It is illegal to copy this book, post it to a website, or distribute it by any other means without permission.

This book is for educational and informational purposes only and does not constitute financial advice. The author and affiliated entities are not financial advisors and assume no liability for investment decisions made by readers. Always consult a qualified fiduciary or licensed professional before investing.

First edition

This book was professionally typeset on Reedsy.
Find out more at reedsy.com

"The universe is a quantum computer."

— Seth Lloyd

Contents

Preface

This book exists because the conversation around quantum computing has evolved, and investors have taken notice.

For years, quantum lived on the fringe of capital markets. It was discussed in research labs, physics journals, and long-range roadmaps. Investors who paid attention were early, but the dominant question was simple and unresolved: will quantum computing ever actually matter? That is no longer the question.

Today, quantum computing is discussed alongside artificial intelligence, energy infrastructure, national security, and large-scale computing systems. It is no longer framed as a distant experiment. It is framed as a necessary future layer for the systems already under construction.

That shift did not happen because quantum suddenly "worked." It happened because AI scaled faster than expected, and classical computing began to show physical, energy, and economic limits.

When the CEO of NVIDIA, Jensen Huang, publicly described quantum as the next major computing platform, investors listened. Not because quantum is ready tomorrow, but because NVIDIA sits at the center of global compute infrastructure. When that company discusses its next steps, markets take notice. This book exists to translate that shift.

Invest AI Quantum established what quantum computing is, why it matters, and who the early leaders are. That foundation still holds. This book does not replace it. It moves forward from it. The questions investors are asking now are different.

Where does quantum show up before it is perfect?
Which companies benefit while timelines remain long?
What does "quantum exposure" actually mean in infrastructure terms?
And how does quantum quietly become part of the systems powering AI, cloud, energy, and defense?

This book is about quantum stacks.
It is about infrastructure, not breakthroughs.
It is about capital alignment, not theory.

And it is about seeing long-term value before it becomes obvious.

Prologue

When *Invest AI Quantum* was written, the world was in a different phase.

At that time, quantum computing was understood as an emerging force. It was real and serious, but still framed as a theory moving toward application. Most timelines placed a meaningful impact fifteen to twenty years away. Investors who paid attention were early, and the conversation was patient. That framing made sense then.

Artificial intelligence was growing, but not at today's pace. Data centers were expanding, but energy and cooling were not yet strategic constraints. Classical computing still felt elastic. The pressure had not arrived. *Invest AI Quantum* was written for that moment.

Book One explains what quantum computing is, why it matters, and who the early leaders are. It builds technological literacy and a long-term perspective. That role has not changed. Book One is still essential. What changed is everything around it.

In a short period of time, AI accelerated faster than forecasts predicted. Models grew larger. Systems became more complex. Power demand surged. Cooling became a bottleneck. Energy reliability became a board-level concern. The limits of classical computing stopped being theoretical and started becoming operational. As a result, quantum moved forward in the conversation.

Not as a replacement for classical machines, not as a miracle breakthrough.
But as a support layer. A missing piece. A technology that does not stand alone, but strengthens the systems already driving economic growth.
This is the moment this book addresses.

This book does not repeat Invest AI Quantum. It builds on it. Where Book One explains what quantum is, this book focuses on how quantum becomes real and where capital aligns while it matures. Together, the two books form a complete arc.

This prologue exists so the reader understands that relationship before Chapter One begins. Book One is the foundation. This book is the infrastructure lens.

With that context set, we move forward.

Introduction

How to Use This Book

Quantum computing is not becoming important because it is impressive. It is becoming important because the systems we already depend on are under strain.

Artificial intelligence is scaling faster than expected. Models are larger, more expensive, and more energy-intensive. Data centers are pushing against power limits. Cooling has become as strategic as processors. At the same time, the problems AI is asked to solve are becoming more complex, involving optimization, simulation, and decision-making at a scale classical systems were not designed to handle indefinitely.

This book starts from that pressure, not from theory.

It does not assume quantum computing arrives suddenly or perfectly. It assumes systems evolve when constraints appear, and capital moves toward what will be needed before solutions are complete. That pattern has repeated across every major infrastructure shift in modern history.

Throughout this book, quantum is treated as part of that pattern. Not as an isolated invention, and not as a replacement for existing technologies, but as something being prepared to work alongside them.

This is not a physics book. It does not attempt to teach quantum mechanics. It is an investment framework designed to help readers understand where quantum computing fits into the future of AI, energy, security, and large-scale systems, and how capital is beginning to organize around that fit.

The chapters that follow are structured to support different investing styles and time horizons. Some readers will use this book to identify long-term positioning themes. Others will use it to understand near-term signals, sector exposure, and where volatility and opportunity may emerge as the stack develops. Many will simply use it to understand what quantum computing actually means for markets today.

Readers who want to move quickly to companies and market exposure can do so. Readers who want to understand why those markets exist will find the structure laid out step by step.

This book is written for active traders, long-term investors, and anyone seeking informed exposure to one of the most important shifts shaping the future of artificial intelligence. It does not require prior technical knowledge, only curiosity and a desire to understand where capital is moving next.

Everything here is educational, not investment advice. It is a lens for understanding how quantum computing is being positioned beneath modern systems before it becomes visible on the surface.

With that context set, Chapter One begins where the market conversation actually shifted.

1

Why Quantum Is Now an Infrastructure Conversation

For a long time, quantum computing was discussed as a future technology. The focus was possibility, not deployment. Could it work, and if it did, when would it matter? That phase has ended.

Today, quantum computing appears in the same conversations as artificial intelligence, energy systems, national security, and large-scale computing infrastructure. That shift happened for a simple reason: the systems being built are encountering real limits.

AI models are larger. Training runs are longer. Energy use is higher. Some of the problems AI is now asked to solve involve so many variables that classical computers struggle to keep up, regardless of incremental performance gains.

When systems reach their limits, markets do not abandon them. They reinforce them.

Quantum computing is not positioned to replace classical computers or artificial intelligence. It is positioned to support them. It functions as an additional layer, assisting with optimization, simulation, materials science, cryptography, and other high-complexity workloads where classical systems alone become inefficient.

That is why quantum is now an infrastructure conversation.

Infrastructure is not about excitement. It is about durability. It is about building systems that allow other systems to grow without collapsing under their own complexity.

Two years ago, quantum was framed primarily as a breakthrough technology. Today, it is framed as a missing layer that becomes more relevant as AI systems expand.

This shift is visible in behavior. Companies are no longer focused solely on building better qubits. They are focused on control, cooling, power stability, integration with GPUs and CPUs, and reliability under real workloads. Governments are funding platforms rather than isolated experiments. Enterprises are exploring access models rather than ownership.

These are signals of maturation.

Invest AI Quantum established why quantum matters and who the early leaders are. This book moves forward. It focuses on how quantum becomes usable, scalable, and investable through systems and stacks rather than isolated moments.

Quantum will not arrive as a single event. It will arrive as infrastructure. And the structure being assembled underneath it is the quantum stack.

2

What the Quantum Stack Means for Investors

Every durable investment theme begins with an authority moment. For quantum, that moment did not come from a lab result. It came from capital attention. When market commentators publicly tied quantum positioning to Jensen Huang's statements, the signal was not about near-term performance. It was about relevance.

When the CEO of NVIDIA enters a conversation, the market understands that a technology has crossed from speculation into infrastructure adjacency. That is how themes mature.

From that point forward, quantum stops being discussed as a single breakthrough and starts being understood as a system. For investors, a quantum stack is the layered architecture that turns fragile quantum hardware into something enterprises can access, integrate, and pay for. Each layer corresponds to real companies, real spending, and visible supply chains already forming in public markets.

At the core of the stack sits quantum compute itself, the processors that perform quantum operations. This includes superconducting systems, trapped-ion machines, neutral atoms, photonics, and quantum annealing. Public exposure appears through pure-play companies such as IonQ (IONQ), Rigetti Computing (RGTI), and D-Wave Quantum (QBTS), alongside diversified technology leaders like IBM (IBM), Alphabet (GOOGL), and Microsoft (MSFT). This layer attracts headlines, but on its own it does not create durability.

Immediately beneath and around it is the physical reality most investors miss. Superconducting quantum machines depend on extreme cryogenics and ultra-stable environments. While leading cryogenic suppliers such as Bluefors are private, the investment implication is clear. As quantum systems scale, demand pulls materials science, precision manufacturing, and thermal engineering supply chains with it. This layer grows regardless of which qubit architecture ultimately dominates.

Control electronics form the next critical layer. Quantum processors require extraordinarily precise timing, RF and microwave control, photonics, clocks, and measurement systems. This is where classical hardware quietly becomes a quantum pick-and-shovel story. Public companies such as Keysight Technologies (KEYS) sit directly in this demand path, supplying the instrumentation and testing capabilities quantum systems cannot function without. This layer monetizes early because quantum machines are unusable without it.

Above control sits error correction, the true gating factor of the entire industry. Markets are already shifting focus away from raw qubit counts toward the race for logical, error-corrected qubits. Error correction relies heavily on classical compute running alongside quantum hardware, reinforcing hybrid architectures. Progress here determines when quantum systems move from experimental to reliable, making this layer one of the most important signals for long-term investors.

Software and developer ecosystems follow naturally. Compilers, SDKs, and orchestration frameworks make quantum systems programmable, portable, and usable. Platforms such as IBM's Qiskit, Google's Cirq, and NVIDIA's CUDA-Qdefine how developers actually interact with quantum hardware. This is also where quantum becomes cloud-native rather than machine-bound, lowering adoption friction and widening access.

Hybrid compute is the gravitational center of the modern quantum stack. Quantum does not replace GPUs or CPUs. It depends on them. Accelerated classical compute handles simulation, optimization, and error decoding alongside quantum processors. This is why NVIDIA's role is structural rather than symbolic. Its position at the intersection of AI acceleration and quantum orchestration explains why Jensen Huang's commentary carries weight with investors.

Cloud delivery defines the enterprise adoption gate. Amazon (AMZN) through AWS Braket, Microsoft through Azure Quantum, and Google through its cloud platforms determine how organizations actually consume quantum computing. Companies rent access, test workloads, and integrate cautiously. This layer governs revenue pacing far more than physics does.

Security and networking expand the stack into national infrastructure. Post-quantum cryptography, quantum key distribution, and secure communications pull defense spending and government contracts into the ecosystem. Space becomes relevant here not as speculation, but as a delivery mechanism for secure quantum communications and sensing, tying quantum investment themes to aerospace and long-cycle public budgets.

Power and energy form the constraint layer beneath everything. Advanced computing is increasingly power-limited. As AI and quantum workloads grow together, stable energy becomes strategic rather than optional. Nuclear energy is now openly discussed as a solution for data-center resilience and baseload stability, drawing utilities, energy developers, and infrastructure providers into the quantum narrative. This is not hype. It is a response to physical limits.

Finally, space completes the outer ring of the stack. Even when quantum computers remain Earth-bound, space matters through secure communications, sensing, defense logistics, and national initiatives. This layer connects quantum to aerospace firms, launch providers, and government programs that operate on decade-long horizons.

This is the quantum investment stack enforced throughout this book. Every chapter maps to one of these layers. Every company earns its place by participating in a real system, not a theoretical one.

Quantum investing is not about picking a winning qubit. It is about understanding how infrastructure forms, where capital flows before consensus, and why companies that support inevitability often outperform those that chase spectacle.

3

From Quantum Breakthroughs to Quantum Systems

For years, the quantum conversation revolved around breakthroughs. Headlines focused on record-setting qubit counts, experimental milestones, and isolated demonstrations of what might one day be possible. Each announcement sounded like progress, and technically, it was. But none of those breakthroughs answered the question that ultimately matters to markets.

Can quantum systems be used reliably, every day, at scale?

A breakthrough proves something can work once. A system proves something can keep working.

Over the past two years, the center of gravity has shifted. Companies are no longer optimizing for impressive results in controlled settings. They are optimizing for uptime, stability, integration, and repeatability. The questions have changed from how to achieve a result to how to sustain one. That shift marks the difference between experimentation and infrastructure.

This distinction matters because durable value is created by systems, not moments. A single quantum result does not change industries. A system that can be accessed, controlled, maintained, and improved year after year does.

Artificial intelligence accelerated this transition. AI does not exist in isolation. It depends on data centers, power availability, cooling capacity, software orchestration, and constant operational oversight. As AI systems scaled, they exposed the reality that advanced computing succeeds only when entire stacks function together. Quantum computing is now being built under that same assumption.

The problems companies are focused on today reflect this new phase. They involve controlling large numbers of qubits with precision, reducing noise and interference, correcting errors fast enough to be useful, and integrating quantum processors into classical workflows. These are not headline problems. They are engineering problems, and engineering problems lead directly to infrastructure.

The tone around quantum has changed as a result. Less spectacle. More patience. Less promise. More planning. That shift is not a loss of momentum. It is a sign of maturation.

When a technology enters its systems phase, timelines extend but outcomes stabilize. Standards begin to form. Governments shift funding from research toward platforms. Enterprises explore access models rather than ownership. Capital moves away from isolated bets and toward layered exposure.

Quantum computing is now in that phase.

This does not mean quantum is close to replacing classical computing. It means quantum is being prepared to support it. The objective is not perfection. It is steady improvement inside a broader computing stack.

Attention is moving away from dramatic announcements and toward quiet construction. Toward companies solving practical constraints. Toward businesses that benefit as the quantum stack takes shape piece by piece.

That transition is not accidental. It is convergence.

4

When Markets Start Talking About Quantum Differently

Markets rarely change their language suddenly. They adjust before the shift becomes obvious.

For a long time, quantum computing lived at the edges of financial discussion. It appeared in research notes and distant forecasts, framed as speculative and far off. That framing is changing.

Quantum is now discussed alongside artificial intelligence, energy infrastructure, and national systems. This does not mean quantum is ready. It means its role is becoming clearer.

Markets do not wait for technologies to be finished. They position around what will be required next.

Artificial intelligence has exposed real constraints. Some problems take too long to compute. Some models consume too much power. As these limits appear, capital looks for reinforcement.

Quantum is being discussed in that context. Not as a replacement for classical computing, but as a supporting layer in a broader computing stack.

This shift in language matters. When quantum is grouped with power, cooling, security, and infrastructure, it signals a move from speculative innovation to system-level planning. System-level technologies attract patient capital. They develop slowly, but they tend to endure.

At this stage, the investor risk is no longer disbelief. It is misallocation.

Not every quantum-related company will succeed, but the ecosystem itself is becoming real. Governments, enterprises, and technology leaders are planning around quantum methods playing a role, even before those methods are fully mature.

For investors, the question is no longer whether quantum matters. It is where value forms during the build. That value often appears in unglamorous places: control systems, energy infrastructure, cooling, orchestration software, and hybrid platforms.

Market language changes first. Capital allocation follows. Structure reveals itself last. Understanding that sequence keeps investors grounded.

5

Why Artificial Intelligence Accelerated the Quantum Timeline

Quantum computing did not speed up on its own. Artificial intelligence pulled it forward.

For many years, quantum computing moved at a steady, careful pace. Progress was real but slow. Research advanced. Hardware improved. Error rates declined. But there was no urgent pressure forcing quantum systems into everyday relevance. Artificial intelligence changed that.

AI systems began growing faster than expected. Models required more data. Training required more computation. Inference required more energy. As AI spread into more industries, the strain on existing computing systems became visible.

Some problems became too large. Some simulations became too slow. These were not failures of AI. They were signs of success. When a system grows, it eventually exposes its limits.

Quantum computing began to matter more not because it suddenly became better, but because the problems AI was trying to solve became harder. Quantum methods are well suited to certain types of problems that classical computers struggle with, especially those involving many possibilities at once.

As AI advanced, the value of those methods increased. This is why the quantum timeline shortened.

The world did not suddenly decide quantum computing was ready. It realized it would eventually need it. That realization shifted priorities. Funding increased. Partnerships expanded. Systems planning began.

This does not mean quantum computing is about to replace AI or classical computing. It means quantum is being prepared to assist them.

For investors, this distinction matters. Technologies that are pulled forward by necessity tend to receive long-term support. They are not treated as optional. They are treated as strategic. Quantum computing is now entering that category.

This is also why quantum is increasingly discussed alongside energy and infrastructure. AI growth places pressure on power systems. Quantum systems add additional requirements. Together, they push planners to think at a system level.

Quantum is no longer a standalone future idea. It is becoming part of a broader response to AI-driven growth.

6

From Theory to Application Without the Hype

When people hear that timelines are shortening, they often assume results are immediate. Foundational technologies do not work that way.

Quantum computing is not suddenly ready for mass use. Error rates remain high and systems are still delicate. What has changed is not capability, but intent.

Two years ago, the conversation centered on whether quantum would ever matter. Today, the focus has shifted to how quantum can be made useful sooner, even in narrow, assisted, or hybrid roles. That shift is critical.

Instead of waiting for ideal machines, companies are deploying partial solutions. Hybrid workflows. Assisted optimization. Targeted applications that integrate quantum methods where classical systems struggle. This is how infrastructure actually forms.

History is consistent on this point. Electric grids were unreliable when first deployed. Early computers were inefficient and expensive. Progress did not come from perfection. It came from systems that existed and improved year after year.

The primary risk for investors is not technological failure. It is narrative distortion. The belief in sudden revolutions, flawless machines, or single-company dominance misreads how infrastructure develops.

The opportunity in quantum is not one winner. It is the gradual construction of a stack, a layered system that becomes more capable over time and increasingly embedded in broader computing workflows.

Understanding this process separates noise from progress. It explains why certain companies benefit long before quantum computers reach full capability and why value often appears outside the headline names.

From here forward, the book leaves theory behind. The focus shifts fully to application, structure, and long-term positioning. The question is no longer whether quantum matters. It is how it integrates into the future of AI, energy, and global systems.

7

Hybrid Computing: Where Quantum and AI Actually Meet

One of the most persistent misunderstandings about quantum computing is the belief that it replaces what already exists. It does not. Quantum does not replace classical computers or artificial intelligence. It works alongside them.

This is where hybrid computing enters the picture.

Hybrid computing means different machines doing different jobs within the same workflow. Classical systems handle general tasks. GPUs power large-scale AI workloads. Quantum systems assist with specific problems that are difficult to solve efficiently using classical methods alone. This is not a future idea. It is the architecture already being built.

Most practical quantum work today happens inside hybrid loops. Classical computers prepare problems and interpret results. Quantum systems explore complex solution spaces. The output returns to classical systems, often repeatedly. The value comes from the interaction, not from any single machine operating in isolation.

This structure changes the adoption curve. Quantum does not need to be perfect to matter. It needs to be useful in narrow, well-defined ways.

As AI systems scale, they increasingly face problems defined by combinatorial explosion, massive state spaces, or optimization limits. These are precisely the areas where quantum methods can assist, even when results are approximate. Hybrid systems allow quantum techniques to contribute without requiring full quantum advantage.

This is why hybrid computing becomes the bridge between experimentation and infrastructure. It allows quantum to enter real workflows early, while machines improve in the background. It also allows capital to flow gradually into software, orchestration, control, and integration layers rather than into a single speculative bet.

Hybrid computing creates economic relevance before technical perfection. It shifts attention away from breakthroughs and toward connection points. The companies that matter most here are often not quantum hardware builders, but the firms that enable systems to work together.

This is where AI and quantum actually meet, not as competitors, but as collaborators inside a layered computing stack.

Understanding this keeps expectations realistic. Quantum adoption will not arrive loudly. It will arrive quietly, as hybrid workflows become standard and quantum assistance becomes normal.

The next chapter moves from architecture to exposure, identifying the companies positioned to benefit from this hybrid future, whether or not they ever build a quantum computer themselves.

8

The Role of Infrastructure Giants in the Quantum Stack

Quantum computing is often framed as a contest between specialized startups and research labs. That framing misses where the real leverage sits. Some of the most important beneficiaries of quantum progress are infrastructure companies that may never build a quantum processor themselves.

Infrastructure companies control the systems new technologies must attach to in order to function. They provide compute, networking, power, control, and integration at scale. When a new computing layer emerges, it does not replace what exists. It plugs into it.

Quantum follows this pattern.

Practical quantum systems depend on classical infrastructure for simulation, calibration, error correction, orchestration, and uptime. They run inside data centers. They rely on existing cloud platforms. They integrate into workflows that enterprises already use. This makes infrastructure giants unavoidable participants in the quantum stack.

Their advantage is not technical novelty. It is system control. These companies understand scale, reliability, and adoption. They do not need to win the qubit race to benefit from quantum becoming usable. Quantum becomes another workload layered into platforms that already generate revenue.

This position lowers risk and stretches timelines in a way long-term investors should recognize. Infrastructure companies can benefit from quantum progress even if hardware advances slowly, because demand appears first in access, integration, and hybrid workflows rather than in standalone machines.

That is why infrastructure leaders speak about quantum in measured terms. They are not promising breakthroughs. They are preparing compatibility. Their objective is to be ready when quantum becomes operational, not to predict when that moment arrives.

History favors this role. Infrastructure companies tend to persist across technology cycles because they absorb innovation rather than betting on a single outcome. In the quantum stack, they form the backbone that allows fragile hardware and experimental methods to function in real environments.

For investors, this shifts the question away from who builds the best quantum computer and toward who controls the systems quantum must run on. That is where durability appears long before consensus forms.

Next, we move down the stack to the physical reality of quantum hardware itself, and why scaling quantum machines remains one of the hardest engineering problems in computing.

9

The Hardware Reality: Why Quantum Is Hard to Build

Quantum computing is powerful in theory and fragile in practice. That fragility is not a footnote. It is the defining constraint.

For investors, this matters because quantum systems are not difficult simply because the math is advanced. They are difficult because the physical world is unforgiving. Qubits are extremely sensitive to heat, noise, vibration, and interference. Small environmental changes can introduce errors. Building a quantum computer is therefore not just about designing a processor. It is about controlling everything around it.

This is why progress can feel slow.

Adding more qubits does not automatically improve a system. In many cases, it makes the problem harder. More qubits mean more signals to control, more noise to suppress, and more points of failure. Raw qubit counts look impressive, but they do not translate directly into usefulness. Stability and control matter more than scale.

As a result, serious hardware teams prioritize quality over size. They spend years refining fabrication methods, materials, and layouts. They work to reduce error rates, improve consistency, and make behavior predictable. These improvements rarely produce dramatic headlines, but they are what determine whether a system can run reliably at all.

Quantum hardware development looks less like consumer electronics and more like aerospace engineering. Precision matters. Testing matters. Margins are tight. There are no shortcuts.

This reality explains why timelines stretch and why progress can appear uneven. Companies pause, restructure, or change direction not because quantum is failing, but because building at the edge of physics demands patience. That patience is a feature, not a flaw.

It also explains why infrastructure support is inseparable from hardware progress. Control electronics, measurement tools, cooling systems, and integration platforms are not optional. They are what allow fragile hardware to function long enough to be useful.

For investors, the hardware challenge is not a reason to dismiss quantum. It is a filter. Technologies that are easy to build attract fast capital and fast competition. Technologies that are hard to build move slower, but often produce deeper moats.

Quantum hardware is difficult because it pushes against real physical limits. That difficulty is not weakness. It is the cost of building something genuinely new.

10

Control, Timing, and the Invisible Electronics Layer

Quantum computers do not run themselves. They are driven, timed, and measured by classical systems that rarely get credit.

Every qubit must be controlled with extreme precision. Signals have to arrive at the right moment, at the right strength, in the right sequence. The system has to read results back quickly and cleanly. If timing drifts, if signals bleed into each other, if measurement gets noisy, the computation collapses. That entire job belongs to the control and measurement layer, the invisible electronics that turns quantum hardware from a science object into a usable machine.

This layer includes control electronics, timing systems, signal generation, readout hardware, and the instruments used to calibrate everything. It is not glamorous, but it is structural. Quantum hardware without control is silence.

Scaling makes this layer harder, not easier. More qubits mean more channels, more coordination, tighter synchronization, and more chances for interference. A single qubit can behave beautifully on a bench. A system of many qubits demands orchestration. Small timing errors can cascade. Measurement errors can disguise progress. Noise can look like randomness until it ruins the outcome.

This is why many performance gains in quantum come from better control rather than better qubits. Cleaner signals, tighter clocks, faster feedback loops, and improved measurement can raise usable performance without changing the core processor. Investors should care because this is one of the most consistent pick-and-shovel areas of the stack. No matter which qubit approach wins, the machine still needs precision electronics and reliable measurement.

This is also where public market mapping becomes practical. Companies such as **Keysight Technologies (KEYS), Analog Devices (ADI), and Texas Instruments (TXN)** sit in the orbit of signal integrity, precision control, and electronics that matter more as quantum systems scale. The point is not that these firms are pure quantum plays. The point is that quantum spending pulls their capabilities forward as part of the stack.

If hardware is the headline, control is the reality. This is one of the layers that gets paid while the industry waits.

In the next chapter, we move into the constraint investors keep underestimating: cooling, energy, and the physical limits that decide whether scaling is even possible.

11

Cooling, Energy, and the Physical Limits of Quantum Systems

Quantum computing does not struggle because the ideas are unclear. It struggles because the physical world is unforgiving.

Most quantum systems only function under extreme conditions. They must operate at temperatures colder than outer space, in environments shielded from vibration, noise, and interference. Heat is not a minor inefficiency. It is a system failure.

Even small amounts of thermal energy can disrupt qubits and destroy results. This is why advanced cooling and environmental control are not optional features. They are the foundation that allows quantum hardware to exist at all.

As systems scale, this challenge intensifies. More qubits require more connections. More connections generate more heat. More heat increases instability. Managing that tradeoff becomes one of the hardest problems in quantum engineering, and one of the clearest constraints on timelines.

This is where energy and cooling stop being background considerations and become first-order limits. Quantum systems run inside facilities that draw continuous power, demand extreme reliability, and cannot tolerate fluctuations. As AI and quantum workloads grow side by side, energy demand compounds and cooling becomes as critical as compute itself.

For investors, this shifts where value forms. Thermal management, power delivery, grid stability, and infrastructure resilience become part of the quantum story whether the market labels them that way or not. These are not speculative add-ons. They are requirements.

This is also where quantum collides with broader infrastructure reality. Data centers already push against grid limits. Quantum systems raise the bar further, pulling energy planning, redundancy, and long-term capacity into the core stack discussion.

Quantum is not constrained by imagination. It is constrained by physics. That is why progress is deliberate and why infrastructure companies matter so early.

In the next chapter, we move from physical limits to the quiet race that determines when quantum becomes reliable at all: error correction.

12

Error Correction: The Real Race No One Sees

Quantum computers fail quietly and often, not because of poor engineering, but because quantum systems are exposed to the smallest disturbances. Heat, noise, timing drift, and even measurement itself can introduce errors. Left unmanaged, those errors compound until computation becomes meaningless. This is why error correction sits at the center of the quantum stack and quietly determines every realistic timeline.

Unlike classical computers, quantum systems cannot copy data and check it later. Instead, they combine many fragile physical qubits into a single, more reliable unit known as a logical qubit. The system continuously monitors for signs of error and corrects them in real time without collapsing the computation. This process is not elegant or fast. It is resource-intensive and unforgiving.

One logical qubit can require many physical qubits, ultra-fast control electronics, precise timing, and significant classical computing power running alongside the quantum machine. This is why error correction, more than raw hardware announcements, determines when quantum becomes usable. Physical qubits show potential. Logical qubits show reliability. The gap between the two is where progress actually lives.

This reality explains why the most serious quantum players focus less on spectacle and more on systems. IBM has been explicit that its roadmap is driven by logical qubits, not qubit counts, integrating error correction across hardware, control electronics, and its Qiskit software stack. Alphabet's quantum work centers on surface codes and scalable correction, even when headline qubit growth appears modest. Microsoft has gone further by structuring its entire quantum thesis around error suppression first, treating error correction as a systems problem rather than a hardware race through Azure Quantum and its topological approach.

Pure-play quantum hardware companies are even more dependent on this layer. IonQ's trapped-ion architecture emphasizes higher-fidelity qubits to reduce correction overhead. Rigetti's superconducting systems require continuous advances in calibration, control, and decoding to remain viable. D-Wave, while using annealing rather than gate-based systems, still depends heavily on classical post-processing and noise management to make hybrid workloads practical.

What is often missed is where the real leverage sits. Error correction is overwhelmingly classical. Decoding errors, managing feedback loops, and coordinating corrections require massive classical compute. This is why NVIDIA sits structurally inside the error-correction race without building quantum hardware. GPUs are critical for real-time decoding and hybrid workflows, making accelerated classical compute a non-optional part of the quantum future. Intel plays a similar role through cryo-CMOS control chips and classical-quantum interfaces designed to reduce latency inside correction loops.

Software completes the picture. Error correction increasingly lives in orchestration layers rather than hardware alone. Improvements in compilers, control software, and system coordination can unlock more usable computation from the same machines. This is why progress often arrives quietly, through refinements that never change the processor but dramatically improve reliability.

For investors, the signal is clear. Error correction is not a product and it will never appear as a clean revenue line. It shows up as slower qubit growth paired with better uptime, improving logical qubit counts, tighter hybrid integration, and calmer language from leadership. Companies that talk less about records and more about reliability are usually further along than they appear.

Quantum computing will not become dependable through a single breakthrough. It will become dependable through thousands of small corrections, applied continuously, until instability turns into routine control. This is the real race, and it is already well underway.

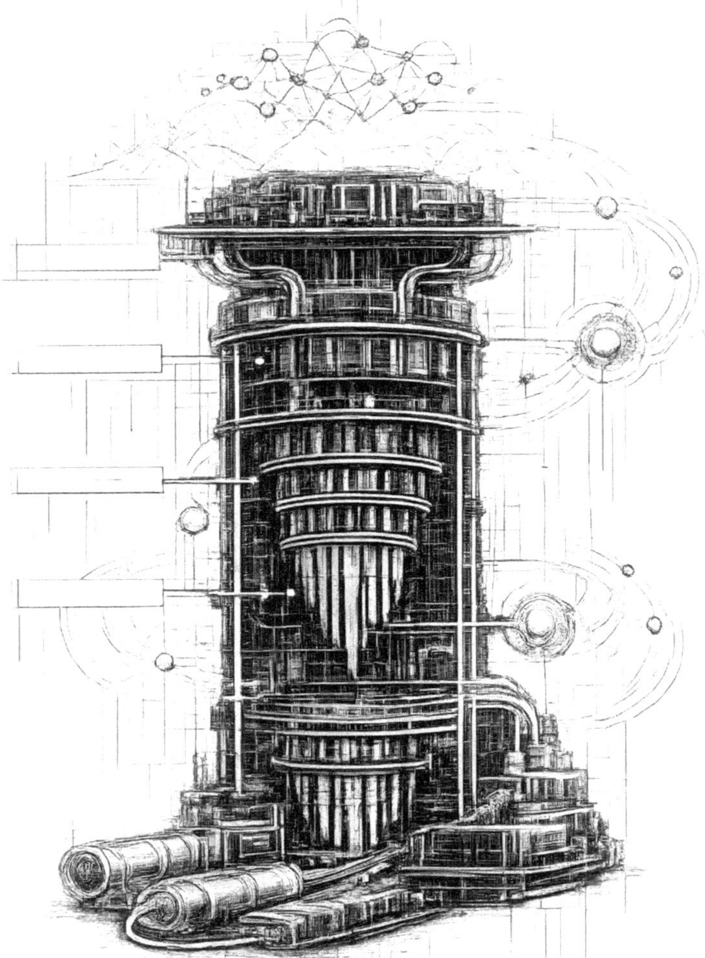

13

Why Software and Orchestration Matter More Than Speed

In every major computing cycle, speed attracts attention, but usability determines winners. Faster machines do not matter if they cannot be coordinated, managed, and integrated into real systems. Quantum computing follows the same rule.

Even the most advanced quantum hardware is ineffective without software that knows how to deploy it. Quantum systems do not operate in isolation. They sit inside workflows that include classical computers, GPUs, data pipelines, and AI models. Software decides when quantum is used, how tasks are split, how errors are handled, and how results return to the broader system.

This orchestration layer is what separates experiments from production. Without it, quantum remains a specialized tool used by experts. With it, quantum becomes part of normal computing behavior.

This is why progress in quantum software often matters more than marginal gains in hardware speed. Better compilers, scheduling, and workflow management can extract more value from existing machines without changing the physics underneath them. Software can reduce friction, improve reliability, and make imperfect systems useful sooner.

For investors, this pattern should feel familiar. Operating systems shaped personal computing. Platforms shaped mobile. Cloud orchestration shaped enterprise IT. In each case, coordination and integration mattered more than raw performance.

Quantum is entering that same phase. Software and orchestration enable hybrid workflows, lower adoption barriers, and allow organizations to experiment without committing to full-scale deployment. They make gradual progress possible and normal.

In the quantum stack, speed is a feature. Orchestration is the foundation.

14

Public Companies by Quantum Stack Layer

One of the most common mistakes investors make with emerging technologies is treating them as a single market. Quantum computing is not one market. It is a stack of markets forming at different speeds, with different risk profiles and different capital behaviors.

Viewing quantum through the stack immediately changes how exposure should be evaluated. The question is no longer which company will "win quantum." The question becomes which layers are being built now, which layers monetize early, and which companies benefit even while the technology matures.

At the most visible layer are companies working directly on quantum hardware. These firms build qubits, fabricate processors, and design quantum systems. Public examples include IonQ, Rigetti Computing, and D-Wave Quantum, alongside diversified technology leaders such as IBM, Alphabet, and Microsoft. This layer offers upside, but it is volatile and tightly linked to technical execution and error correction progress.

Beneath and around hardware sits infrastructure, where many investors underestimate value formation. These companies do not build qubits, but quantum systems cannot function without them. Control, timing, and measurement companies such as Keysight Technologies supply precision electronics that every quantum architecture requires. Cooling, power management, and integration firms participate regardless of which hardware approach succeeds. These businesses tend to have diversified revenue bases and benefit from quantum scaling without depending on breakthroughs.

Another layer focuses on software, orchestration, and access. This is where quantum becomes usable rather than experimental. Cloud and hybrid platforms provided by Amazon, Microsoft, Alphabet, and NVIDIA determine how enterprises actually interact with quantum systems. Their value grows as quantum integrates into existing workflows, even when hardware progress is incremental.

Seeing companies by stack layer reframes risk and durability. Hardware exposure offers asymmetric upside but higher uncertainty. Infrastructure exposure offers steadier demand tied to system construction. Software and platform exposure offers leverage across many use cases as adoption spreads.

This layered view also explains why certain companies appear repeatedly in quantum discussions despite not branding themselves as quantum companies. They occupy positions that become more valuable as systems mature and hybrid computing becomes normal.

Quantum investing is not about speed. It is about placement. Understanding public companies through the quantum stack allows investors to see where capital forms gradually, across layers, rather than all at once.

That is how durable exposure is built.

15

The Non-Obvious Beneficiaries of Quantum Growth

When new technologies emerge, attention usually concentrates on the most visible players. In quantum computing, that attention tends to follow companies building qubits or announcing experimental milestones. History suggests that this focus is often misplaced.

The strongest long-term beneficiaries are usually the suppliers. They are the companies that provide what every system needs, regardless of which design ultimately wins.

Quantum computing does not scale on breakthroughs alone. It scales on infrastructure. Power, cooling, precision electronics, measurement systems, and software integration are not optional layers. They are required for any quantum system to function, improve, or remain stable. These requirements grow steadily as systems mature, independent of headlines or technical hype.

Cooling and thermal management are an early example. As quantum systems increase in size and complexity, heat and environmental stability become limiting factors. Even small expansions intensify thermal challenges, turning advanced cooling from a support function into a core dependency.

Control and measurement occupy a similar position. Every quantum architecture depends on precise timing, low-noise signaling, and accurate readout. These demands do not disappear if one qubit technology outperforms another. They persist across superconducting, trapped-ion, photonic, and annealing approaches.

Energy infrastructure sits beneath all of it. Quantum systems require stable, high-quality power, and those requirements grow as quantum and artificial intelligence workloads expand together. Power reliability becomes a strategic constraint rather than a background assumption.

Software and orchestration complete the picture. Hybrid systems only become usable when complexity is managed and access is simplified. These tools allow experimentation, integration, and gradual adoption without requiring full commitment or perfect hardware.

These companies rarely sound futuristic. That practicality is their advantage. For long-term investors, non-obvious beneficiaries offer exposure to quantum growth without depending on uncertain technical inflection points or winner-take-all outcomes.

Instead of betting on which quantum computer wins, this layer of the stack supports inevitability. It is where value accumulates quietly while attention remains elsewhere.

16

Private Infrastructure Leaders Shaping the Stack

Public markets show only the surface of quantum development. Much of the real construction happens privately, years before it appears in earnings calls, product launches, or stock charts.

Private infrastructure companies focus on narrow but essential problems inside the quantum stack. They build dilution refrigerators, cryogenic wiring, control hardware, calibration systems, and error-correction tooling that quantum machines cannot function without. Their work is technical, specialized, and largely invisible to the public.

Companies such as Bluefors dominate ultra-low-temperature refrigeration used in superconducting quantum systems. Firms like Oxford Instruments supply cryogenic environments, measurement tools, and laboratory infrastructure that underpin both academic and commercial quantum programs. In control and instrumentation, private and semi-private suppliers feed precision electronics and timing systems into nearly every major quantum lab and platform.

Other private players focus on software layers that never show up as standalone products. Error-mitigation libraries, calibration automation, and orchestration tooling are often developed quietly and embedded directly into enterprise platforms operated by larger public companies. These firms do not compete for headlines. They solve problems deeply enough that larger ecosystems depend on them.

Their customers are not consumers. They are governments, defense agencies, research institutions, and large technology companies. Their timelines follow engineering cycles rather than quarterly reporting cycles. Success is measured in system stability, uptime, and reproducibility, not user growth or brand recognition.

This private layer absorbs risk early. It is where experimentation happens when outcomes are uncertain and payoffs are distant. When solutions prove durable, they are acquired, partnered with, or folded into public platforms without ceremony. By the time investors see progress reflected in public companies, much of the hard work has already been done.

This dynamic explains why quantum progress can appear sudden. Years of private iteration precede visible adoption. When infrastructure stabilizes, applications scale quickly, and the beneficiaries are usually public companies positioned to integrate what private firms have already validated.

Private infrastructure leaders operate beneath the noise by design. They move slowly because physics demands it, and decisively because systems depend on it.

Quantum development feels quiet until the stack locks into place.

17

Quantum ETFs and Structured Exposure

Many readers want one simple question answered. Is there an ETF for quantum computing?

The most widely known example is the **Defiance Quantum ETF (QTUM)**. QTUM tracks an index that includes companies tied to quantum computing and machine learning, and its holdings are publicly available. This makes it a useful reference point for how the market currently defines quantum exposure.

That definition is rarely pure-play. Quantum exposure through ETFs usually blends quantum and AI. This is not a flaw. It reflects reality. The early monetization path for quantum is hybrid, and many enabling companies support both ecosystems.

From an educational standpoint, an ETF like QTUM can function as a map rather than a recommendation. Even without investing in it, readers can study the holdings to see which companies are grouped into the quantum theme and how different layers of the stack appear at the market level.

This is where long-term thinking matters.

Learning the quantum stack means understanding both the technology and how markets package that technology into products. Studying ETFs shows how themes become investable before they become mature.

This book does not tell anyone what to buy. It shows how quantum becomes structured, labeled, and understood by markets as an emerging investment theme.

Understanding that structure is the first step toward clarity.

18

Why Quantum Is a 10-Year Investment, Not a Trade

Quantum computing does not behave like most market narratives. It does not reward speed, react cleanly to headlines, or move in straight lines. That is because quantum is not a product cycle. It is an infrastructure cycle.

Foundational technologies create value by becoming necessary, not by moving quickly. Roads, power grids, and communication networks did not reward traders who chased moments. They rewarded investors who understood structure early. Quantum is following the same path.

This is why quantum belongs on a ten-year horizon.

Short-term volatility will be constant. Stocks will surge and retrace. Announcements will overpromise and underdeliver. None of that alters the underlying reality that quantum systems are still being assembled layer by layer. For investors, the challenge is psychological. Quantum feels early, yet its relevance is no longer theoretical.

That tension tempts people to trade headlines instead of tracking construction. This book argues against that instinct.

A long-term view does not eliminate risk. It reframes it. Progress in quantum will be uneven by design. Some years will look quiet. Others will feel noisy. The signal is not momentum. It is continuity.

Are systems becoming more stable year over year? Are error rates falling across architectures? Are hybrid workflows moving from experiments into routine use? Are infrastructure layers attracting sustained capital?

These are the signals that matter.

Quantum will not produce clean, short-term returns because it is not built for that purpose. It offers exposure to a structural shift in how complex problems are approached, optimized, and solved. That exposure only becomes meaningful when time is allowed to work.

Quantum investing feels uncomfortable for traders because patience is required before validation arrives. For long-term investors, that discomfort is the entry point.

Quantum is not late. It is early, deliberate, and already under construction.

19

The Three Phases of Quantum Adoption

Quantum computing will not arrive all at once. It will arrive in phases.

Understanding these phases replaces guesswork with structure. Each phase has different goals, signals, and expectations.

The first phase is stack formation. This is where quantum stands today.

During this phase, the focus is on building layers. Hardware improves slowly. Control systems become more precise. Error correction advances step by step. Hybrid workflows begin to appear. Infrastructure expands quietly. This phase is not about widespread use. It is about readiness.

Progress here often feels invisible to the public, but it is tangible to engineers and institutions. Investment during this phase is about identifying who is building foundations, not who is selling finished products.

The second phase is integration.

This phase begins when quantum systems appear regularly inside real workflows. Not as standalone machines, but as helpers. Quantum assists AI models, optimization tools, and simulations. Access improves. Software hides complexity. Value forms through connection and orchestration rather than performance alone.

The third phase is lock-in.

This phase arrives when quantum capabilities become difficult to replace. Industries depend on them for specific tasks. Standards form. Systems stabilize. Quantum earns its place as infrastructure.

Lock-in does not mean dominance. It means dependence. Each phase builds on the last.

Confusion comes from forcing later-phase expectations onto earlier phases. Clarity comes from recognizing where we are.

Quantum computing is firmly in the first phase, with early signs of the second beginning to appear. That is a healthy position.

For long-term investors, phase awareness matters more than prediction. The question is not how fast quantum arrives, but whether progress matches the phase.

That distinction turns patience into discipline.

20

What Long-Term Investors Actually Track: How Short-Term Investors and Day Traders Can Use the Same Signals

Long-term investors, short-term investors, and day traders are not playing different games. They are playing the same game on different clocks.

Quantum computing can feel confusing because it does not move in clean cycles. There are no product launches that flip a switch from failure to success. Progress shows up structurally, often long before it shows up in revenue. That makes quantum difficult to trade blindly, but powerful to engage with intentionally at any horizon.

Long-term investors use this framework to understand direction. Short-term investors and day traders use it to understand context, risk, and timing. The signals are the same. The application is different.

One of the most important signals across all timeframes is continuity. Are companies committing capital year after year, even when headlines fade? Are governments maintaining funding through quiet periods? Are partnerships still forming during drawdowns and sentiment resets? Continuity reduces the probability that a theme disappears. For long-term investors, it supports conviction. For traders, it helps distinguish temporary volatility from structural breakdown.

Another shared signal is system improvement rather than headline metrics. Raw qubit counts generate excitement, but they are not the most actionable indicator. Improvements in error rates, control accuracy, uptime, and access matter more. These gains often surface indirectly through expanded cloud availability, software updates, infrastructure spending, or integration announcements. Long-term investors read this as maturation. Short-term investors and day traders can read it as confirmation or invalidation of narrative-driven moves.

Hybrid adoption is a third signal that matters across styles. When quantum tools begin appearing inside AI workflows, optimization pipelines, or research platforms, usefulness is emerging even without perfect machines. For long-term investors, this signals early phase transition. For active participants, it helps identify when attention is shifting from speculation toward application, often before price fully reflects it.

Infrastructure expansion provides another layer of insight. Growth in cooling capacity, control electronics, power planning, and secure access suggests expectation of scale. Infrastructure investments are rarely made for technologies expected to stall. Long-term investors view this as foundation building. Short-term investors and day traders can view it as reinforcement that downside narratives may be overstated.

Language is the final signal. Early-stage technologies are discussed in visionary terms. As systems mature, the language shifts toward integration, reliability, cost, and timelines. That shift often precedes changes in capital behavior. It matters whether someone is holding for years or positioning around sentiment and volatility.

This framework does not prescribe a single strategy. It provides situational awareness.

Long-term investors use it to stay aligned with structural reality rather than noise. Short-term investors and day traders use it to understand whether moves are driven by hype, transition, or genuine system progress.

Quantum computing does not reward guessing. It rewards understanding.

The quantum stack gives that understanding to anyone willing to read it correctly, regardless of time horizon.

21

The Invest AI Quantum Stack

Future-Forward Companies, Infrastructure, and Exposure Map
(Educational, Theoretical, and Speculative — Not Investment Advice)

Disclaimer: This chapter is for educational and informational purposes only. It does not constitute investment advice, financial advice, or a recommendation to buy or sell any securities. All examples are illustrative and speculative. Readers should consult a licensed fiduciary or financial advisor before making any investment decisions.

This chapter exists because theory without direction is incomplete.

This stack reflects the author's and Invest AI's core operating framework for understanding quantum exposure; a more exhaustive and expanded mapping of companies, layers, and adjacent systems appears in the appendix and across the broader Invest AI series, including Invest AI Quantum, Invest AI Robotics, Invest AI Crypto, and Invest AI: The Last Gold Rush.

The purpose of Invest AI has always been to map the future early, not just describe it. In the chapters before this one, we explained how quantum computing moved from theory to systems, how it now supports artificial intelligence, and why infrastructure matters more than hype. Now we show the reader where the stack lives in the real world.

This is the future-forward quantum stack, laid out from top to bottom.

Layer 1: Quantum + AI Integration Giants
(Hybrid Compute, Orchestration, Platforms)
These companies sit at the intersection of AI, classical computing, and quantum integration. They do not need quantum to "win" in order to benefit from it.

- NVIDIA (NVDA)
- GPUs, CUDA-Q, hybrid orchestration, quantum simulation, error-correction acceleration
-
- Microsoft (MSFT)
- Azure Quantum, orchestration, enterprise access layer
-
- Alphabet (GOOGL)
- Google Quantum AI, AI-quantum research, infrastructure integration
-
- IBM (IBM)
- Full-stack quantum systems, enterprise delivery, standards leadership
-

- Amazon (AMZN)
- Braket platform, access layer, hybrid cloud delivery

Why this layer matters: This is where quantum becomes usable before it is perfect.

Layer 2: Pure-Play & Near-Pure Quantum Hardware Companies
(Higher Risk, Higher Upside)
These companies focus on building quantum computers themselves.

- IonQ (IONQ)
- Trapped-ion systems, fidelity-first approach
-
- Rigetti Computing (RGTI)
- Superconducting qubits, vertically integrated approach
-
- D-Wave Quantum (QBTS)
- Optimization-focused quantum systems
-
- Quantum Computing Inc. (QUBT)
- Quantum-adjacent systems and tooling

Why this layer matters: This is where breakthrough risk lives. These companies are sensitive to technical progress and timelines.

Layer 3: Control, Measurement, and Precision Electronics
(The Invisible Toll Booth)
Every quantum computer, regardless of design, needs this layer.

- Keysight Technologies (KEYS)
- Quantum control and readout systems
-
- Teradyne (TER)
- Precision testing, instrumentation, and automation
-
- Analog Devices (ADI)
- Low-noise signal chains and timing
-
- Texas Instruments (TXN)
- Precision analog and control components

Why this layer matters: Quantum cannot scale without control. This layer benefits regardless of which qubit wins.

Layer 4: Cooling, Cryogenics, and Thermal Infrastructure
(The Physical Reality Layer)Quantum computing is limited by heat and stability, not ambition.

Public / Public-Adjacent

- Oxford Instruments (OXIG.L)
- Dilution refrigerators and quantum cryogenics
-
- Chart Industries (GTLS)
- Industrial-scale cryogenic systems
-
- Private (Infrastructure Leaders)
- Bluefors
- Leading dilution refrigerator systems for quantum labs

Why this layer matters: No cooling = no quantum system. Period.

Layer 5: Energy, Nuclear, and Power Stability

(The Quiet Accelerator)

As AI and quantum grow together, power quality and stability become strategic.

- BWX Technologies (BWXT)
- Nuclear components and advanced reactors
-
- GE Vernova (GEV)
- Grid systems, power stability, energy infrastructure
-
- NuScale Power (SMR)
- Small modular reactor exposure
-

Why this layer matters: Quantum systems cannot scale on unstable grids.

Layer 6: Defense, Space, and Quantum Sensing

(National-Scale Adoption)

Quantum enters infrastructure lock-in first through defense and sensing.

- Lockheed Martin (LMT)
-
- Northrop Grumman (NOC)
-
- L3Harris Technologies (LHX)

Why this layer matters: Defense adoption signals permanence, not hype.

Layer 7: Quantum & AI ETFs
(Structured Exposure)

- Defiance Quantum ETF (QTUM)
  Tracks companies tied to quantum computing and machine learning

Why this layer matters: ETFs reveal how markets currently bundle the theme.

Bonus Exposure: Adjacent Future Systems
(See, Appendix)

Robotics automation (ABB, Siemens)
Quantum-adjacent crypto research (post-quantum cryptography themes)

AI infrastructure convergence

22

Conclusion

Quantum computing will not arrive with a single announcement. It will arrive the way infrastructure always arrives, quietly, by becoming normal before it becomes famous.

The signal was never one perfect machine. It was the stack taking shape in public. Control systems improving. Error correction moving from theory into engineering. Cloud access becoming routine. Hybrid workflows tightening the bond between GPUs, AI systems, and quantum accelerators. Power and cooling turning into first-order constraints that pull energy, grid stability, and long-cycle infrastructure into the conversation. When those pieces start forming together, something real is happening.

That is the purpose of this book. Not to predict a date. Not to sell a miracle. But to show where the money trail forms before the consensus story catches up.

If you only watch quantum headlines, you miss the build. The real progress spreads across companies that may never call themselves quantum companies at all, yet still get paid as quantum becomes usable. This is why waiting for certainty so often means arriving late, paying more, and competing with the crowd rather than thinking ahead of it.

Quantum is not a replacement technology. It is a systems response to necessity. Artificial intelligence is scaling into limits of power, complexity, and computation that classical systems alone cannot manage forever. The response is not one breakthrough. It is a layered computing era. Quantum becomes one of those layers, working alongside AI, infrastructure, energy, and national systems.

This is why quantum investing is not about picking a winning qubit. It is about understanding how infrastructure forms, how capital flows before comfort sets in, and why companies that support inevitability often outperform those that chase spectacle.

The quantum stack is forming now. Not loudly. Not cleanly. But deliberately.

For readers who want to go deeper without getting lost in noise, the appendix provides a broader tracking map of stack layers, companies, and signals to watch as the next decade unfolds, along with references to the wider Invest AI series for expanded context.

This book exists so you can see what is being built while it is still under construction.

What you do with that view is your decision. But the build is real, and it is already underway.

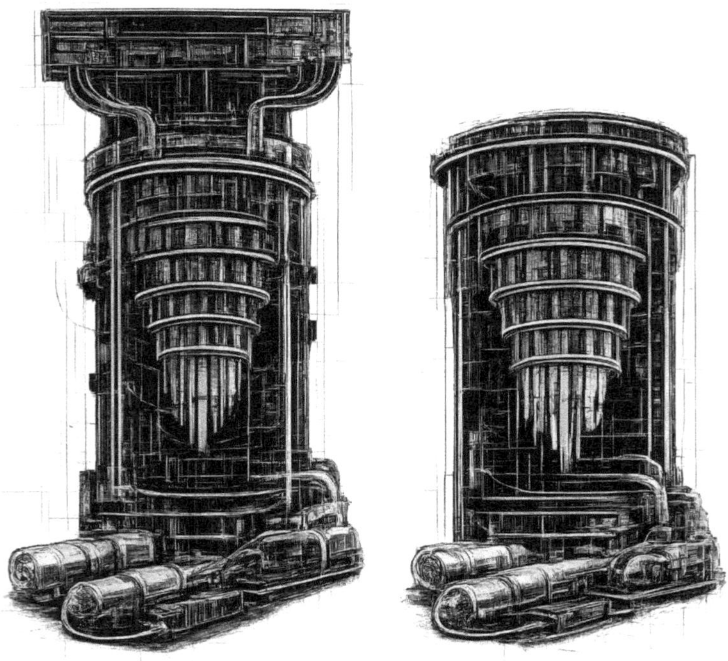

APPENDIX: The Invest AI Quantum Stack

The Invest AI Quantum Stack (Clean Framework)

APPLICATIONS & USE CASES

Optimization • AI assistance • Simulation

▲

SOFTWARE & ORCHESTRATION

Hybrid workflows • Cloud access

Compilers • Scheduling • Error handling

▲

CONTROL, TIMING, & MEASUREMENT
Precision electronics • Readout systems
RF • Photonics • Clocks

▲

QUANTUM COMPUTE CORE (QPU)
Superconducting • Trapped ion
Neutral atom • Photonic • Annealing

▲

COOLING & CRYOGENIC REALITY
Dilution refrigeration • Thermal control
Environmental stability

▲

ENERGY, POWER, & SYSTEM STABILITY

Grid quality • Advanced nuclear
Backup power • Resilience

▲

DEFENSE, SPACE, & NATIONAL ADOPTION
Security • Communications • Sensing
Long-cycle government lock-in

APPENDIX: Quick-Reference Spread (Investor Cheat Sheet)

Educational and speculative. Not investment advice.

1. HYBRID COMPUTE & INTEGRATION
Platform layer that benefits first

NVIDIA (NVDA)
IBM (IBM)
Microsoft (MSFT)
Alphabet / Google (GOOGL)
Amazon / AWS (AMZN)

2. QUANTUM HARDWARE (PURE-PLAY RISK)
Higher volatility, higher narrative risk

IonQ (IONQ)
Rigetti Computing (RGTI)
D-Wave Quantum (QBTS)
IBM (IBM)
Alphabet / Google (GOOGL)

3. CONTROL, TIMING, & MEASUREMENT
Pick-and-shovel layer

Keysight Technologies (KEYS)
Analog Devices (ADI)
Texas Instruments (TXN)
Teledyne Technologies (TDY)
Amphenol (APH)

4. COOLING & CRYOGENICS
Physical gatekeeper of quantum scale

Oxford Instruments (OXIG.L)
Bluefors (Private, industry standard)
Chart Industries (GTLS)
Linde (LIN)

5. ENERGY, NUCLEAR, & GRID STABILITY
AI + Quantum = power constraint

BWX Technologies (BWXT)
GE Vernova (GEV)
Duke Energy (DUK)
NextEra Energy (NEE)

6. DEFENSE, SPACE, & LOCK-IN ADOPTION
Long-cycle government demand

Lockheed Martin (LMT)
Northrop Grumman (NOC)
RTX (RTX)

| Boeing (BA) |
| L3Harris Technologies (LHX) |

7. THEMATIC & BASKET EXPOSURE |
Diversified access to the theme |

| Defiance Quantum ETF (QTUM) |
| ARK Autonomous & Robotics ETF (ARKQ) |

APPENDIX: Top Public Companies by Invest AI Quantum Stack Layer

SUMMARY

The listed companies are real, publicly verifiable entities with legitimate exposure,

participation, or adjacency to the quantum investment stack as it exists today.

There are NO fabricated companies and NO hallucinated tickers.

Important distinction:

This is an INVESTMENT STACK, not a physics purity list.

Some companies have direct quantum revenue today.

Others are infrastructure, orchestration, or system beneficiaries.

That distinction is intentional and correct.

APPLICATIONS & USE CASES

IBM (IBM) – Verified quantum + enterprise optimization and hybrid workloads

Alphabet (GOOGL) – Verified AI, simulation, materials science, Cirq ecosystem

Microsoft (MSFT) – Verified enterprise AI + quantum integration

Amazon (AMZN) – Verified optimization and hybrid workloads via

AWS

Palantir (PLTR) – Verified AI-driven optimization and government use cases

ANSYS (ANSS) – Verified simulation software benefiting from quantum acceleration

Dassault Systèmes (DASTY) – Verified engineering and simulation platforms

Cadence Design Systems (CDNS) – Verified advanced modeling and optimization

Synopsys (SNPS) – Verified semiconductor and system simulation

SAP (SAP) – Verified enterprise optimization and logistics software

SOFTWARE & ORCHESTRATION

——————————-

NVIDIA (NVDA) – Verified CUDA-Q hybrid GPU/QPU orchestration

IBM (IBM) – Verified Qiskit quantum software stack

Microsoft (MSFT) – Verified Azure Quantum orchestration

Amazon (AMZN) – Verified AWS Braket access and orchestration

Alphabet (GOOGL) – Verified Cirq quantum software tooling

Intel (INTC) – Verified quantum control and integration tooling

AMD (AMD) – Verified accelerated compute adjacency

Oracle (ORCL) – Verified enterprise cloud orchestration (adjacent)

Snowflake (SNOW) – Verified data orchestration adjacency

ServiceNow (NOW) – Verified workflow orchestration at scale

CONTROL, TIMING, & MEASUREMENT

————————————

Keysight Technologies (KEYS) – Verified RF, timing, and quantum control

Teledyne Technologies (TDY) – Verified measurement and sensing

Teradyne (TER) – Verified test and precision electronics

National Instruments (NATI) – Verified test and measurement (now owned by Emerson)

Analog Devices (ADI) – Verified precision signal processing

Texas Instruments (TXN) – Verified control electronics

Microchip Technology (MCHP) – Verified timing and control ICs

Marvell Technology (MRVL) – Verified high-speed interconnects

Broadcom (AVGO) – Verified precision networking and RF

Lattice Semiconductor (LSCC) – Verified control logic

QUANTUM COMPUTE CORE (QPU)

———————————————

IonQ (IONQ) – Verified trapped-ion quantum systems

Rigetti Computing (RGTI) – Verified superconducting QPUs

D-Wave Quantum (QBTS) – Verified annealing and hybrid systems

IBM (IBM) – Verified superconducting quantum roadmap

Alphabet (GOOGL) – Verified superconducting quantum research systems

Microsoft (MSFT) – Verified topological and neutral-atom direction

Intel (INTC) – Verified quantum hardware research

Honeywell (HON) – Verified Quantinuum exposure via legacy stake

Amazon (AMZN) – Verified Ocelot quantum chip research

Alibaba (BABA) – Verified quantum research exposure

COOLING & CRYOGENIC REALITY

———————————————-

Linde (LIN) – Verified industrial gases and cryogenics

Air Products & Chemicals (APD) – Verified cryogenic infrastructure
Chart Industries (GTLS) – Verified cryogenic systems
Parker-Hannifin (PH) – Verified thermal and fluid control
Emerson Electric (EMR) – Verified industrial automation and cooling
Johnson Controls (JCI) – Verified thermal management systems
Trane Technologies (TT) – Verified data center cooling
Vertiv Holdings (VRT) – Verified data center thermal infrastructure
Carrier Global (CARR) – Verified advanced cooling systems
Siemens (SIEGY) – Verified industrial thermal systems

ENERGY, POWER, & SYSTEM STABILITY

———————————————————

Constellation Energy (CEG) – Verified nuclear power for data centers
NextEra Energy (NEE) – Verified grid-scale energy
Duke Energy (DUK) – Verified grid stability
Exelon (EXC) – Verified nuclear and grid exposure
Brookfield Renewable (BEPC) – Verified power infrastructure
Dominion Energy (D) – Verified nuclear and grid assets
GE Vernova (GEV) – Verified power systems and grid technology
Siemens Energy (SMNEY) – Verified power infrastructure
Schneider Electric (SBGSY) – Verified power management
Eaton (ETN) – Verified electrical resilience

DEFENSE, SPACE, & NATIONAL ADOPTION

—————————————————————-

Lockheed Martin (LMT) – Verified defense and quantum sensing
Northrop Grumman (NOC) – Verified national security systems
Raytheon Technologies (RTX) – Verified defense electronics
Boeing (BA) – Verified aerospace and secure systems

L3Harris Technologies (LHX) – Verified secure communications

General Dynamics (GD) – Verified defense infrastructure

Palantir (PLTR) – Verified government AI and analytics

Kratos Defense (KTOS) – Verified space and defense technology

Iridium Communications (IRDM) – Verified satellite communications

Maxar Technologies – Verified geospatial and defense (private)

Appendix: How to Track the Quantum Stack Over Time

Most investors struggle with future technologies not because they are too early, but because they watch the wrong signals.

When a technology is truly emerging, the most important changes do not appear in headlines. They appear in language, spending patterns, and structural decisions that are easy to miss if attention stays on price movement or press releases.

One early signal is executive language. In the earliest phase, conversations are visionary. Leaders talk about breakthroughs and possibilities. As systems mature, language shifts toward integration, reliability, and coordination. When discussions become operational, focused on uptime, standards, and deployment, it signals preparation for permanence.

Capital allocation tells a similar story. Infrastructure scales through commitment, not excitement. New laboratories, expanded cooling facilities, power agreements, and government-backed contracts matter more than optimistic forecasts. These investments are slow, expensive, and deliberate. When they appear consistently, they reflect long-term intent.

Another signal is how quantum capabilities appear inside other tools. Quantum rarely arrives as a standalone product. It shows up as assistance. It helps optimize AI models, improve simulations, refine logistics, or accelerate materials discovery. When quantum methods are embedded rather than advertised, usefulness has already begun.

Error correction progress is one of the most overlooked indicators. Headlines often focus on qubit counts, but stability matters more than size. Logical qubits matter more than physical ones. Consistency over time matters more than peak performance. When reliability improves steadily, the stack becomes usable, even without dramatic announcements.

Government and defense adoption is another signal worth tracking. These institutions move slowly, but once they commit, they commit for long horizons. Their involvement often marks a shift from experimental to strategic.

Looking further ahead, subtler signals suggest where the stack may evolve. One is the convergence between quantum systems and power optimization. As AI workloads grow, energy efficiency becomes a constraint. Quantum-assisted optimization in scheduling, materials, and thermal management may be among the earliest areas of broad impact.

Another signal lies in hybrid architectures. The future is layered. Classical systems handle scale. Quantum systems handle complexity. AI orchestrates between them. Progress in orchestration and hybrid control frameworks may prove as important as advances in hardware.

There is also growing, quieter attention on secure communication and system integrity. As global systems become more interconnected, resilience and trust rise in importance. Investments here often precede public recognition by many years.

Quantum investing is not about being early. It is about not being blind. This book does not tell you what to buy. It teaches you how to see.

Once you recognize how the stack forms and reinforces itself over time, it becomes difficult to view the future of AI, energy, and global systems the same way again.

The stack reveals itself slowly. Once it does, it tends to remain.

Appendix: A Long-View Bonus: Where AI, Robotics, Crypto, and Quantum-Driven Systems May Converge

This section exists as a reference point, not a recommendation.

Over the next decade, the most influential companies across artificial intelligence, robotics, crypto, and quantum-driven systems are unlikely to announce themselves all at once. Many will already be familiar. Others will feel peripheral until the systems they support become essential. What matters here is not prediction, but orientation.

In artificial intelligence, long-term influence increasingly comes from platforms, infrastructure, and orchestration layers rather than models alone. Companies such as NVIDIA, Microsoft, Alphabet, Amazon, and Meta Platforms shape how AI scales through compute, cloud infrastructure, developer ecosystems, and deployment. Over time, their importance shifts from novelty to permanence.

Robotics unfolds more slowly, but with deeper physical consequences. Robotics is where AI leaves the screen and enters the world. Companies like Tesla represent long-term bets on autonomy and embodied intelligence, while firms such as ABB and Fanuc quietly embed automation into factories, logistics, and infrastructure. Progress here favors reliability over visibility.

Crypto occupies a different role. Over long horizons, its relevance is less about speculation and more about coordination, settlement, and trust. Platforms such as Coinbase function as gateways rather than endpoints, while networks like Ethereum operate as programmable infrastructure. Crypto tends to matter most where verification, interoperability, and decentralization are required.

Quantum-driven systems sit at the intersection of these domains. Companies such as IBM, Google, and Intel explore quantum-adjacent architectures while supporting classical systems that will coexist with quantum methods for many years. Quantum influence is likely to appear first through optimization, simulation, and system-level assistance rather than consumer-facing products.

For readers wondering where participation begins, access matters more than sophistication. Platforms such as Robinhood, Webull, and Moomoo provide visibility into public markets and capital flows as these technologies evolve. They are not strategies, but observation points.

This appendix is not a map of what will win. It is a snapshot of where attention often gathers before systems mature. Over long horizons, leadership is shaped less by hype than by execution, integration, and endurance.

The goal here is not instruction. It is awareness. In a world where systems evolve faster than intuition, seeing clearly is already an advantage.

www.ingramcontent.com/pod-product-compliance
Lightning Source LLC
LaVergne TN
LVHW050922210926
848482LV00012B/503
* 9 7 9 8 2 9 5 5 5 7 8 0 4 *